SURVIVAL
SONGS

SURVIVAL SONGS

Meggie C. Royer

Fameless Publishing Group, LLC. *New Jersey.*

Library of Congress Cataloging-in-Publication Data

Royer, Meggie C.
Survival Songs / Meggie C. Royer
ISBN-13: 978-0615871592 (Fameless Publishing Group)

BOOK DESIGN BY BRIAN FELIX

CONTENTS

SURVIVAL
SONGS

I

Obsessions

ON HAVING A BOYFRIEND WITH OCD

He was always turning the lights on and off,
opening and closing the door, counting as he went:
thirty-six, thirty-seven, thirty-eight, thirty-nine, forty.
Eventually I had to tell him that if he kept opening the door,
we'd have a whole bunch of house intruders
before the night was through. He responded by trying to kiss me once,
then ended up kissing me twenty-three times, then once more
for an even twenty-four. Then he had to redo two of them
because "our mouths hadn't been quite aligned."
Some nights I'd wake up with the moon soaking the bedsheets,
listening to the sound of him repeating the word "fuck"
over and over: he'd stubbed his toe on the bathroom doorway
but couldn't stop swearing once he'd started.
I fell back asleep after staring at my pillow
until the floral pattern burned into my eyelids,
dreamt the two of us went to an opera but instead of beautiful,
tremulous voices rising high into the air,
two sopranos were singing "fuck" to the tune of La Traviata.
He apologizes the next day, says the new medication
made him feel like shit all the time so he took himself off it;
I respond that it probably made him feel that way
because it was working.
Two days later the ambulance comes and takes him away;
he'd accidentally cut one of his wrists with the steak knife
chopping carrots for stew
but couldn't have just one cut wrist;
he had to have two.

II

Compulsions

THE ELEPHANT IN THE ROOM

My brother is in a relationship with food and it's complicated.
He goes on juice cleanses every other week, claiming the Vitamin C
from all the citrus nutrient shakes are good for him, are a replacement
for sunlight, will prevent him from turning into the vampire he
never wanted to be.
We come from a long line of uncles and grandfathers who taught the men
in our family that muscled six packs were six steps to freedom,
that words like "pecs" and "biceps" were the Holy Grail,
words they led my brother in praying over at family reunions.
At the dinner table, he pushes around mashed potatoes and collard greens
on his plate like a wifebeater who's forgotten how to touch his spouse
in any way other than with a closed fist.
Calories are something he spends more time obsessing over than his girlfriend,
treats them to romantic dates spent leaning over the toilet bowl,
whispers curses like love poems whenever he's ingested too many of them.
My brother's culinary relationship is the elephant in the room,
but he won't stop trying to turn himself into the mouse.
He counts his bites methodically, chews with precision,
engages in midnight runs on the treadmill where the number of miles
his feet travel is more precious to him than any sleep.
Afterwards, he trains himself to drift off in bed by counting calories
instead of sheep. This is his bedtime ritual; it has replaced
even masturbating or brushing his teeth.
He has been taught by my parents that shrinking like plastic

wrap
is a woman's job, but he has never backed down from a
challenge.
My brother is in a relationship with food and it's complicated.
No matter how many times he tries to break up with it,
it always slashes his tires and shows up on his backstep
begging for more.

III

Reminders

FOR TWENTY–YEAR–OLDS WHO HAVE NEVER BEEN LOVED

All of a sudden two decades have passed and you still have not kissed anyone with tongue, or kissed anyone at all for that matter, or had a 3 AM conversation with someone who would rather look into your eyes for ten minutes straight than talk. You have never worn a lover's sweater or "forgotten" it at home in your bedroom just so you would have an excuse to see them again. You have never even stood face-to-face with someone who makes your hands shake so hard it feels like they're both having a separate anxiety attack.

This causes you much guilt and self-blame and sadness but above all, an overwhelming curiosity. Are you really that ugly, that unwanted, that uninteresting, that boring, that no one, absolutely no one, has ever looked at you like the only thing on earth?

The answer is no. The better answer is that someone out there, somewhere in the world, is "wondering what it's like to meet someone like you," and they have two decades worth of love stored in their veins like a shoot-'em-up drug, and they're just about ready to inject it into someone else's bloodstream. All you have to do is roll up your sleeves and wait for it to happen. At times you felt so lonely you could stand at the edge of a cliff with nothing beneath you but air and grass and a long, long way down, and you'd still feel emptier than that canyon itself. Maybe you even danced with yourself alone in your room a few times, arms outstretched around a ghost, pretending someone else's hands were on your waist, someone else's eyes boring into yours.

Or maybe you fell temporarily in love with strangers on public transportation, fell in love with anybody who so much as accidentally brushed your hand on the way past. For you, falling in love with dozens of people a day was a coping mechanism for not having anyone to love you in return. But people are not eggs and falling in love with a dozen of them does not mean your shell will remain uncracked. One day you're going to hit the point where you're so desperate for human contact that you're going to snap in half and all your love will bleed out like egg yolk.

But someone out there is eating a bowl of Ramen noodles right now, or putting on slippers, or settling into bed. They are doing all the normal things that you've done in your own life. They are just like you. They have cellulite and extra fat in all the wrong places and goals and fears and doubts and bad handwriting.

The truth is that they are just like you, and being just like you, they're looking for a lover too. They're what you might call a soulmate. They think they're all alone in feeling the way they do, but you're really both two halves of a whole.

And one day you'll meet them, bump into them on the street, and your two halves will be put together, and you'll make one.

THINGS MY MOTHER DIDN'T TELL ME BUT SHOULD HAVE

Never give any kind of pleasure to a boy you wouldn't give
yourself.
Kiss like a promise and wait for the other person to break it.
Human beings are not ships; you cannot save them from sinking
if they don't want to be rescued from the floodwaters.
Loving someone that doesn't give a damn about you
isn't sexy; it's misplaced energy, also known as
self-destruction.
Don't ever treat anyone like a refugee from a civil war;
they will come back from battle and leave you as wounded
as if you were the one who had been paid
for military service. Forgiveness isn't putting the weapon down;
it's learning how to kiss the person pulling the trigger,
not just a quick peck on the cheek, but a full one with tongue.
Let the dead be dead.
They have no answering machines, no phonelines:
if you call them, only the ground will ring.
Never trust a boy who already has a pack of condoms ready
in his coat pocket before he even asks your name.
When the world tries to break your back with its weight,
get a stronger spine.
Your father left us because he was ashamed
for not being the one that gave birth to you.
Even oceans misplace their anchors sometimes.
Never "give a man permission."
You shouldn't have to. It should be mutual.
Stop treating your body like currency-
don't pay anyone who doesn't deserve it.

REMINDERS TO WOMEN
WITH DEAD HEARTS

For women who have trouble learning how to stop
sharpening their knuckles on the blade of a man's body,
remember that he is not always the shooting star.
Sometimes he is the comet that was named after you
and will smash into earth destroying everything.
Maybe it's time to stop being sentimental
about things like beer and one-night stands
and start remembering the nights that you
actually remember because you weren't blacked out.
Self-forgiveness isn't always about getting the tattoo
that will stay when no one else does;
sometimes it's about getting the tattoo
that hurts the most to ink.

IV

Coping Mechanisms

LOVE POEM ABOUT A COUPLE IN A PSYCH WARD

Tell me that when you inhaled my hair something other
than self-hatred escaped from it and flew into your lungs.
You are who you were before I met you, before we learned
the necessary sadness of convincing our own cells
they were impermeable and could not hold any more water.
You were my impermeability.
You were all the mornings I stood on a rooftop without
jumping.
In the beginning we exchanged each other for matches,
burned them into being on one another's hands.
We fed each other flame like acrobats.
There was nothing about survival that was easy,
but we tricked each other into believing
it could eventually become a habit.

THE YEAR OF LIMITED SILENCES

The year I grew homesick for my own body was the same year
the local police station put a limit on the number of silences
we could hand out, so we started treating our words like mints
and placed them on everyone else's tongues.
We told people we despised that we loved them, cowards
that they were brave. That was the year I caught myself
communicating with whales instead of human beings
because the pattern of their grunts sounded more like quiet.
They gulped tiny schools of fish down like stars.
I gulped down other peoples' silences, as rare as they were,
like throat lozenges. They could have been peach or
honey-lemon
or tomato-flavored and I would not have cared.
That was the year I learned the Inuits had over 50 words
for snow, and felt saddened because they only used two of them
when they didn't even have a limit on their daily number of
silences.
We started kissing the people who came to us with open mouths
filled with secrets
just so we would not have to hear their life stories.
We learned to miss the time when words meant more.
That was the year the person I loved, loved the most,
came to me with the words I love you, but I was so sick of
hearing noise
that I turned away.

DATING A MUTUAL GHOST

The spring after we both killed ourselves,
you with a boxcutter to the wrists and I by leaping off the roof
of your business partner's fourteen-story office, the crocuses
came up as usual, yellow tongues like saxophones poking
through the earth. When you arrived to pick me up, I answered
the door in my underwear since ghosts have no need
for either clothing or modesty. You stood on your tiptoes
to kiss me, and when our mouths touched we felt
that old familiar wound of self-pity.
At the tattoo parlor so you could get the vertical scars
on your wrists inked back on in a stronger color, the artist
would not let a dead couple through his door.
I pleaded with him that we would tell no one else,
that we were not like the usual dead, not scary,
not like zombies or bloody gang members, but to no avail.
At the café where we next stopped for raspberry lattes,
the other patrons stared at us without inhibition,
searched the air for the smell of rot.
There was none.
Later, at home after the movie in which everyone left
to sit in another theater after we entered the doors,
you gave me a bouquet of flowers that wilted in my hands
as soon as I touched them. We were lovers
that had lived and died together, and our date ended as
they always had in life: with both of us trying not to cry,
looking at the floor and wishing we could be more
than our shared self-hatred.

THERE SHOULD BE AN UGLIER NAME FOR UNREQUITED LOVE

When I see the creases in his bed, I imagine what she
must look like sleeping between them, if he ever finds strands
of her long red hair tucked between the sheets and mistakes
them for blood. If hearts could be operated on in the emergency
room by special doctors, well, then, stitch me up.
His name will be my newspaper headline for weeks on end
and I try so hard to pronounce it without hers immediately
following;
drinking to forget someone should be a new kind
of drinking game: for every time they love someone else,
take a Jello shot. Even hangovers feel like a headache's ghost
when compared to this sledgehammer of an ache,
like a piledriver shoved between a whale's ribs
or a suicide bomber's blast decimating the packed earth.
No matter how many men I meet at the bars,
their pickup lines will never compare to what his
must have been the first time he tried to hook up with her.
As a gift for myself whenever they go out on dates,
I buy a new little black dress from the most expensive
clothes store in town, even though I've yet to find
someone else to wear it for.
Pretty soon I'll need a new closet.

V

Same Love

FOR BOYS WHO HAVE BEEN MISTAKEN FOR GIRLS

When they tell you your voice is too high, too whiny, evokes images
of unicorns and pink braided friendship bracelets, that maybe
you should tone it down a notch, tell them that at least you
have vocal cords that are used for good. When they try
to snatch away your towel in the gym locker room to peek
at what's underneath, remind yourself that undressing someone
as a joke is nowhere near undressing someone out of love.
One day someone will remove your clothes because they want
to get as close to you as possible without any layers in between,
instead of trying to get access to your "goods."
On the days when self-doubt feels heavy like a swallowed
peach pit in the bottom of your stomach that you just can't
throw up,
go watch a thunderstorm make its way across the horizon
and convince yourself that you are as full of strength and noise
as the thunderclaps themselves.
You are lightning.
You are bravery in a body that is still learning how to find itself,
like a package that's been mailed to the next door neighbor
instead of to the intended recipient.
When they pull your long hair and laugh about how
they should have brought rubber bands to braid it into pigtails,
stop wishing you could tie it into a noose.
Instead, make a lasso from it and learn how to capture
every shred of self-doubt still floating through your veins,
then throw every last scrap in the garbage can.
You are lightning.
And lightning will always be lightning, no matter
how many times it's been mistaken for anything else.

NOT SO MUCH FALLING IN LOVE AS LEAPING INTO IT

In January my older brother Paul came out without even saying
a single word;
I found him wrapped around the body of another boy in the
kitchen
when he thought everyone else in the house was asleep,
the two of them slow dancing through the light of the open
fridge,
a bag of nectarines rotting sweetly on the marble counter, leak-
ing
dark red sludge like the inner contents of Paul's heart.
In New York City last year a woman was killed while
stargazing,
leaning out the window of her apartment to admire the deep
pink sky
at the same time a young girl above her leapt from her
apartment window,
hitting the woman beneath her, the two of them
plummeting to the earth below, limbs tangled in a lover's
embrace.
And that night as I watched Paul tap out a message on the other
boy's back
in Morse code at the rate of one letter every five seconds,
dash dot dash dash, dash dash dash, dot dot dash,
I realized that the act of falling in love is not so much a falling
as a desperate, terrifying leap off the highest building around,
the kind of jump that ends in not just a single casualty,
but two.

SHOPLIFTING LOVE

The first time I measured your palms against my thighs, I did
so with the intent
of not getting caught. Found my way around your body like a
mall forty minutes
before closing time, anxious with heavy breath, as if someone
had hooked my heart
on a string and tossed it into the center aisle as bait for the store
clerk.
We rolled around in your bed like sardines, attempting to kiss
one another so hard
that we swallowed our tongues like peach pits.
When the door started to creak open on its rusty hinges,
hinges my father had promised we would oil months ago,
its sound was an alarm, a warning signal like the white plastic
tags stuck onto clothes
that spray ink like squid when torn from the fabric.
We removed ourselves from that bed so fast you'd have thought
the cops had come
to shake its pockets down to search for stolen goods.
When he came into the room, I hid the scent of your body in the
space between
my gums and teeth like a shoplifted key, hoping I would have
the chance
to open your double doors again sometime.
We wouldn't have to be so worried about getting caught
if we weren't both girls.

VI

Haphephobia

SURVIVOR'S GUILT

She inhales trigger warnings like oxygen, only goes out in day-
light
for fear of being caught in a dark parking lot by herself.
Her friends, who don't know, tease her and call her the opposite
of a vampire. In the beginning, the cops bagged her evidence
like coin collectors, made bets on which piece of clothing
would give him away first. At home she washed each and every
pair of underwear twice on spin cycle, then scrubbed them out
by hand with soap like they did in the old days,
even though the only truly dirty pair was encased in a plastic
bag.
The term "spoiled goods" ran through her bloodstream
like heroin; she felt it bubbling up in her veins
whenever any other man looked at her like a souvenir,
a stuffed bear's head to put on a plaque on his living room wall.
Now she cradles blame in her arms like an unwanted child born
to a teenage mother, close to her heart, the same heart whose
roots
grew from forgiveness but have yet to burst through the ceiling
of dirt.
Oysters are more at home in their shells than she is in her own
body.
Today, whenever she sees a line of boys in the school cafeteria,
she opens her legs automatically as a reflex,
as if remembering how the men took turns in the parking lot
like they thought each one was better than the last.

AN OPEN PLEA TO JERRY SANDUSKY

I wonder if the rush you got when one of your players lobbed a football

through the goalpost was equivalent to the rush that spread through your veins

after one of those many forced blowjobs.

You know, forgiveness is a heavy thing. It doesn't have a punchline.

Gifts and free tickets to games cannot erase blame, because blame, like Cupid,

always has a target, and you deserve to be hit with every single arrow.

In the newspapers they said you'd written your own law

for how to treat all the young boys that stayed overnight at your house,

and one of the rules was to tell the truth.

Your definition of truth must be what a fortune teller says to a client

when she tells them she can actually read their future with 100% accuracy.

When they grew homesick and wanted to leave your basement, did you muffle their screams and banish them back into their throats

like the ghosts of their ancestors? Did the soundproof walls cradle their whimpers like a sympathetic lover?

Bones break the same way no matter how you set them.

Graves cannot vomit out their dead like purged meals.

Footballs can't turn around once they've sailed through the goalpost.

What you did cannot be undone.

I wonder if all those boys will see your face in place of their partner's

the next time they have sex, if they will feel your wet tongue inside their mouth instead of the person's they love.

You are their infinite trigger warning.

And once a gun's hammer is cocked, there's no stopping it from firing.

POEM FOR THE BOY WHO CALLED ME A SLUT

It's not really any of your business how many bodies
I've waded through knee-deep like water since I grew old enough
to know what sex was, or how many condoms
I've bought in the middle of the night at Costco
with shades on so the clerk wouldn't recognize me.
When I turned eleven, my mother unwrapped a box
of maxi pads like a gift and taught me that every time
a girl bleeds, it's just her body's way
of leaking its beauty from the inside out.
A girl is not a piece of meat;
a girl is more like a piece of ripe fruit.
She might be sour or she might be sweet
but what she wants to do with you
is her choice and you can't unpeel her
without her permission. I wish I could leave
a box of rotten pears on your doorstep for a May Day basket
just to teach you this lesson,
or pull open your jeans just to see who would be
the "slut" then. You'd want it, I bet.
With your fingers in my hair, you'd want it.
Last time I checked, how much sex a girl has
doesn't justify a label slapped on her
like a soup can. And have you ever been on a bus
where men whistle at you or make catcalls
and try to feel you up as you walk to your seat?
You either have or I'm the Queen of England.
The girls at my day camp in eleventh grade
had bright pink hair and wore shorts as tiny
as Barbie doll clothing, and enjoyed sex as much
as the next person.
And guess what you call a woman who enjoys sex?
Nothing but her first name.

AFTER A STRING OF BAD BOYFRIENDS

At seventeen the first one pressed himself up against you
with the force of a hurricane and threw rotten mangos
at your window the night after you refused to go down on him.
But you were always just a long shot, the woman with a heart
like that trick at the doctor's office, the one where the knee
is tapped with the hammer and it jumps like a kite string—
no matter how many times you were hit, your heart kicked back.
Two black eyes and six tubes of concealer later,
the drugstore clerks finally stopped asking what was wrong.
Then the dark-haired poet at twenty, who drank for breakfast,
lunch, and dinner, and never had the patience to remove your
clothes
for any purpose other than performing an act that required
a condom. At twenty-three, you learned the meaning
of the word spare: hand-me-down lover for a butcher
with ten other women in his bed that he treated just like meat.
You spent several months trying to rinse the men out
of your mouth, scrub their hands from your bones
trace your way back to the sea. At twenty-seven you forgot
what men's faces looked like without jail bars in front of them.
It was a relief at thirty to finally find one who didn't
pronounce your name like he was wondering what his
would sound like immediately after it.

ALL THE PSYCHOLOGY TEXTBOOKS SAY REPRESSION DOESN'T EXIST

Two months ago the body of a dead girl was dragged from the bottom
of a lake in Canada, her long red hair getting tangled up
in the fingers of the fishermen who rescued her. One later informed
the local media that he swore he'd felt her heartbeat beneath
his frantic hands, trying over and over again to compress her chest
without cracking her ribs. The coroner later determined that it was not
a heartbeat, but a tiny octopus growing in between her lungs,
rising with the weight of her adolescent breasts. When I read this story
in the newspapers, I thought of you, how you never liked me
to see you naked, how you hid the length of your body beneath the sheets,
how it was always a joy to catch a glimpse
of your shoulders, milk-white, as you let the t-shirt drop to the floor.
Even now I still undress out of habit whenever I meet another man
with the same name as you. It's become a problem.
In my dreams, I'm watching TV or eating lunch at a small cafe,
and there is a man named Michael ordering at the counter, and suddenly
I must remove my dress.
The psychiatrist says it's a defense mechanism, a form of repression,
but I've always wondered
if maybe you had something hidden growing beneath your ribs too.

VII

Crisis Management

A DOCTOR'S OFFICE AND SUICIDE HOTLINE ARE APPROXIMATELY THE SAME THING

The doctor asks me to point to the sadness scale on the wall
to demonstrate how much I miss you, 1 being the lowest:
fine and dandy. I put my finger over the 10, the one that stands
for
I want to find the nearest bridge and jump off it.
He taps my knee with the hammer.
Instead, my heart is the one that responds.
My mother once told me that I learned to walk before crawling,
that I would stumble through doorways, through kitchens,
through neighbors' gardens, sleepwalking at night,
stacking their books neatly in the sink,
leaving plates spilling from the living room shelves.
Now, thirteen and a half years later, I begin to wonder
whether Death has a living room, and if he has nicknamed it
the dying room instead.
The moon only rises on the nights when I call up the suicide
hotline
to say hello. They know my first, middle, and last name by
heart.
I ask for Laura, the one whose voice sounds like a mixture of
honey and gravel.
What's wrong today? she asks.
I forgot how to live, I respond.
On the other end of the line, her soft breathing,
the miles and miles of wire stretching between us,
cigarettes on some faraway street being lit
between cupped hands, an exhale in the night,
two naked bodies spooned together like two halves of an

orange,
and through it all Laura's pauses are busy forming
constellations,
the kind that drowning men hang above their beds.

LETTER TO MY FUTURE DAUGHTER WHEN SHE WANTS TO KILL HERSELF

Someday I hope you'll remove all the butterflies from your stomach
and count them up one by one, then place them in a manila envelope
to keep for all the times you need to feel something;
then you can let them free again. I wish you knew that loneliness
is a hell of a lot like soft-serve ice cream: it can be soothing
when you get it in small doses, but when you take too large
of a serving, you'll end up making yourself sick.
Sometimes your body feels like a sunrise that hasn't started
making its way out of the sky yet, but I promise you
that every ray of sun has to start somewhere,
even buried in the ground with the dirt and the insects,
so deep someone has to dig it out.
But someday someone is going to buy 20,000 shovels
and every single one is gonna be for you,
and they'll bring every ray of sun, every cloud, to the surface
again.
Honey, God himself probably bragged to the angels
when he created you, and even Satan
would want you to remain on Earth
so he could watch you from above and admire your beauty.
I know your heart feels so heavy sometimes that it's
weighing down your throat like all those stones
in Virginia Woolf's pockets, but that's just the heaviness
of a heart that knows how to love
pretty damn much better than anybody else.
If there were a crash course in learning how to not hate yourself
at school, I'd want you to have the best teacher
in the entire world. Every time you take another pill

is another second you could have for getting better.
Every step you take to the top of the rooftop
is another step you could have taken
to get yourself back down.
And I know this self-hatred is luggage over the carrying capacity
at the airport, but someday you'll learn how to remove
all the items you don't need from its suitcases,
and stop breaking your back with its load.
There's a reason God made humans with hands.
It's so that every time they fall,
they can pick themselves back up again.